Stitch/Style
Country
Collection

Stitch Style
Country
Collection

FABULOUS FABRIC SEWING PROJECTS & IDEAS

MARGARET ROWAN

D&C

David and Charles

CONTENTS

INTRODUCTION

Step inside my *Country Collection*, full of beautiful ideas for practical projects, all using fabrics from Joel Dewberry's and Amy Butler's latest wonderful collections. It was so difficult to choose from their sublime fabrics. There is a unique blend of floral and geometric designs from both collections and I enjoyed combining the two styles, for example in the Keep-It-Cosy Draught Excluder. This one will definitely spend the colder months keeping me warm against those chilly draughts!

Joel Dewberry's collection, *Botanique*, is simply gorgeous, featuring a myriad of differing ideas and contrasting influences from French Provençal florals to Mosaic Bloom with its North African Islamic style geometry, both seen in beautiful terracotta on the floor cushion.

To provide you with even more delights to feast your eyes upon I chose from Amy Butler's *Hapi* collection. With its joyous array of vibrant jewel colours, the Lazy Lap Quilt would cheer anyone on a gloomy winter evening.

Change Your Style!

Check out the Change Your Style! pages of the book to see how you can create a completely different look and feel with the same project but using an alternative material The amazing thing about creating accessories for your home is that you can truly make them yours with the fabric choices you make. No one else will ever have one exactly the same!

Country Collections will inspire you to make imaginative and creative projects and the Change Your Style! pages will hopefully show you how projects can be adapted simply by switching the fabrics. Let your own creativity take over and see where it leads you!

Margaret Rowan

Tool Kit

You will be able to make most of the projects in this book with just a basic sewing kit but good quality items and a few extra accessories like the ones shown here will help you to achieve a professional finish.

Machine sewing

- Sewing machine
- Adjustable zipper foot
- Quilting foot

Cutting fabric

- Rotary cutter
- Cutting mat
- Fabric scissors
- Embroidery scissors
- Pinking shears

Measuring fabric

- Transparent measuring grid
- Yardstick
- Ruler

Other

- Needles (for hand stitching)
- Quilting safety pins
- Pattern paper
- Sewing/chalk pencil
- Pins
- Bulldog clip

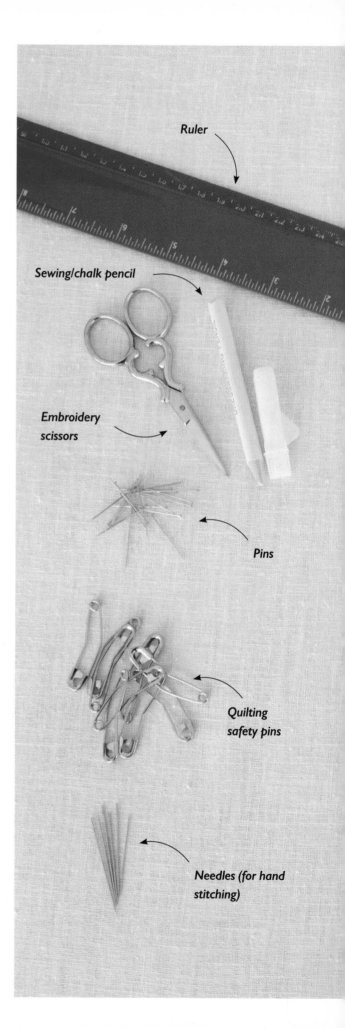

Ruler

Sewing/chalk pencil

Embroidery scissors

Pins

Quilting safety pins

Needles (for hand stitching)

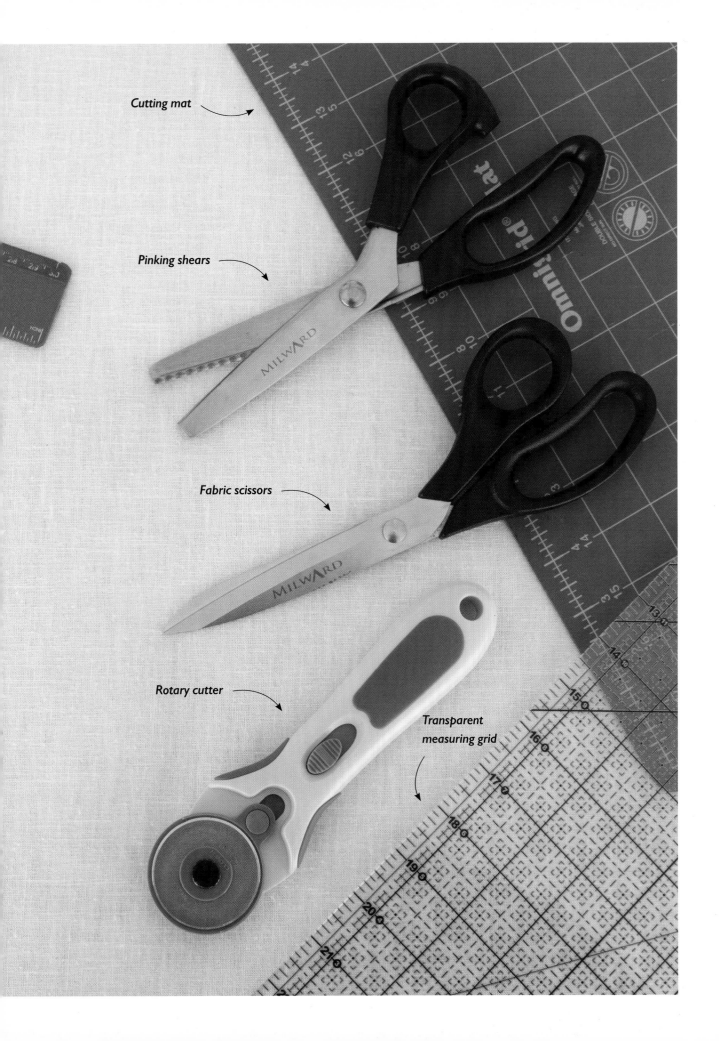

Cutting mat

Pinking shears

Fabric scissors

Rotary cutter

Transparent
measuring grid

JOEL DEWBERRY'S BOTANIQUE COLLECTION

I love the diverse designs found in Joel Dewberry's Botanique collection. The French inspired floral prints work brilliantly against the stronger geometrics in Mosaic Bloom, Houndstooth and Domino. The colours are a wonderful blend of navy and terracotta, ochre and turquoise – a joy to work with!

Mosaic Bloom in Deep Water

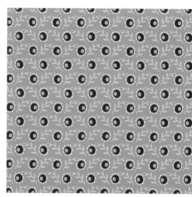

Camelia in Apricot

Bold Bouquet in Asparagus

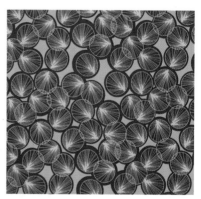

Bold Bouquet in Deep Water

Bold Bouquet in Deep Water

Provençal in Sunset

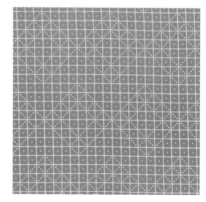

Domino in Sunset

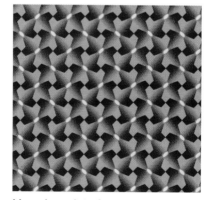

Houndstooth in Asparagus

Lily Pad in Butter

Mosaic Bloom in Sunset

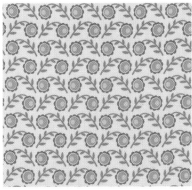

Camelia in Butter

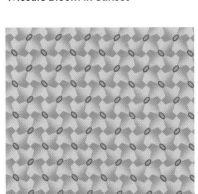

Houndstooth in Butter

Aztec in Teal

Mosaic Bloom in Teal

Bold Bouquet in Teal

Amy Butler's Hapi Collection

This stunning collection from Amy Butler is so inspiring. The colours are strong and beautiful. Again, we have florals and geometric designs along with flowing paisley-like prints in jewel colours. Every part of each design is perfection!

Oasis in Ocean

Oasis in Honeysuckle

Heart Bloom in Rose

Tapestry Rose in Sapphire

Flowering Buds in Emerald

Camel Blanket in Blush

Camel Blanket in Cloud

Glow in Navy

Oasis in Riverstone

Oasis in Azure

Sunflowers in Leaf

Filigree in Bamboo

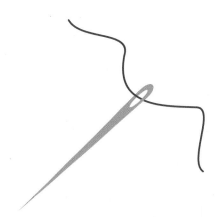

Time-for-Tea Tablecloth

TIME-FOR-TEA TABLECLOTH

You've baked a cake, the pot is brewing so all that's left is to make sure that your table is laid to perfection! A handmade tablecloth is so quick and easy to whip up but is sure to impress your guests, and provides the perfect finishing touch to a beautiful afternoon tea. Why not make coordinating napkins to complete the look?

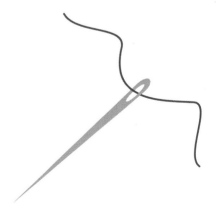

YOU WILL NEED

The finished tablecloth will measure 190cm (75in)

in diameter

- 470cm (185in) of **Mosaic Bloom** in *Deep Water*
- 470cm (185in) of **Lily Pad** in *Deep Water*
- Coats Cotton thread no. 6236
- Chalk pencil
- String

Preparation time

30 minutes

Sewing time

3 hours

TIP

*Fnger press the seam open
before turning the tablecoth
through for a neat, crisp finish.*

Mosaic Bloom in Deep Water

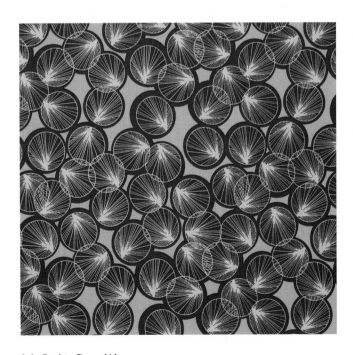

Lily Pad in Deep Water

PREPARING YOUR FABRIC

Cutting the fabric

There is a 1.5cm (⅝in) seam allowance included on the pattern.

- Cut two 235cm (92½in) lengths of Mosaic Bloom.

- Cut two 235cm (92½in) lengths of Lily Pad.

MAKING THE TABLECLOTH

1. Cut one piece of Mosaic Bloom in half vertically and place them either side of the other whole piece, right sides (RS) facing. Fold back the selvedge to line up and match the pattern, pin and tack (baste) in place. Stitch the seams and press open.

2. Fold in half, matching the seams, and then fold into quarters. Make sure that the folds are not creased and are neatly lined up. Pin together both straight sides of the quarter, from the centre to the edges.

3. Pin a piece of string firmly at the the point of the corner (this is the centre of the tablecloth). Tie a chalk pencil to the other end. Keeping the string taught and the pencil vertical, draw the arc of a circle from one folded edge to the other. Cut around this arc (Fig. 1).

4. Repeat steps 1-3 with the Lily Pad fabric.

5. Place the Mosaic Bloom piece and the Lily Pad piece RS facing, matching the seams. Pin and machine stitch around the edge of the cloth, leaving a 10cm (4in) opening to turn the tablecloth through. Stitch across this opening with a large length machine stitch.

6. Press open the seam around the edge and remove the large stitches at the opening. Turn the tablecloth through to the RS and press (Fig. 2). Close the opening with ladder or slip stitch. Pin a line 5cm (2in) from the edge and topstitch using a 3mm (⅛in) stitch length on the machine to give a neat finish (Fig. 3).

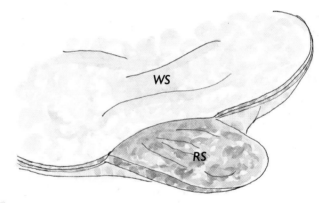

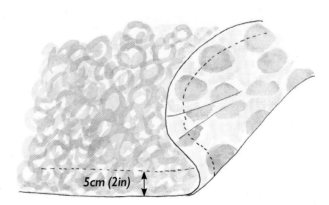

Fig. 2

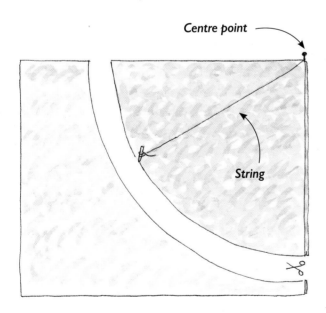

Fig. 1

Fig. 3

CHANGE YOUR STYLE!

Completely transform your kitchen into a luxurious oasis of stylish dining with Amy Butler's richly decorated Oasis fabric. Follow the tablecloth instructions to create small round napkins or placemats in a matching design – just adjust the diameter of the circles to fit.

Change Your Style using Amy Butler Hapi, Oasis in Honeysuckle and Oasis in Ocean.

Fabric Coil Bowl

FABRIC COIL BOWL

Ornamental containers can be surprisingly useful when put in the right place. A thoughtfully positioned bowl in the hallway or on the kitchen counter is the perfect solution for catching those essential small items that are liable to go missing — keys, phone, post. Alternatively, fill them with yummy fruit or bread.

Whatever you use yours for, this coil-work bowl will be a joy. So simple to make, but lovingly handmade to make an impression!

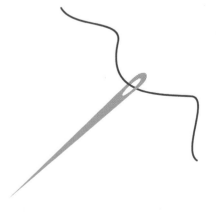

YOU WILL NEED

The finished bowl will measure 30cm (12in) across and 10cm (4in) high

- 100cm (39⅓in) of **Mosaic Bloom** in *Sunset*
- 100cm (39⅓in) of **Provençal** in *Sunset*
- 25m (82ft) of 3mm cord
- Coats cotton thread in white
- Measuring grid
- Bulldog clip

Preparation Time

1 hour

Sewing Time

3 hours

TIP

Check the fabric is cut straight across the width. If it isn't, pull a weft thread across between the selvedges and cut to straighten. Use this edge to find the true bias.

Mosaic Bloom in Sunset

Provençal in Sunset

MAKING YOUR BOWL

1. Take the Mosaic Bloom and fold the selvedge at a right angle to create a bias edge. Crease and cut along the fold (Fig. 1).

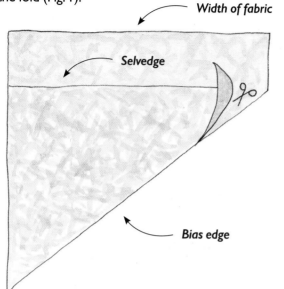

Fig. 1

2. With a measuring grid, cut 3cm (1¼in) wide strips parallel to the bias edge. Cut enough to provide 30m (98½ft) of strips (Fig 2). There is no need to join the strips. 100cm (39⅓in) of fabric will cover approx. 70cm (27½in) of piping cord.

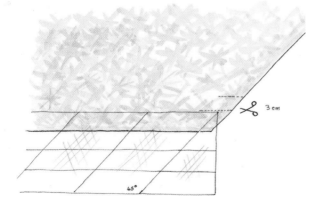

Fig. 2

3. Wrap the first strip over the end of the cord (Fig. 3) and wrap the fabric around the cord at a 45 degree angle (Fig. 4). Keep wrapping the length of the cord and when you reach the end of the strip secure the fabric with a small bulldog clip.

Fig. 3

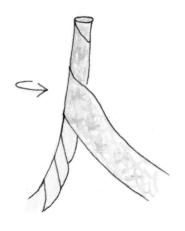

Fig. 4

4. To make the flat base of the bowl, fold over the top of the cord and begin by sewing from the fold with a reverse stitch. Continue in a wide zigzag stitch to the short end of the cord. Try to keep the zigzag in the middle of the two sides (Fig. 5) with the needle catching each side as it zigzags. Starting is a little tricky, be careful not to catch your fingers. Use a couple of large pins to push the short end of the cord to the long end and start turning the cord to create a coil. You may need to raise the presser foot to adjust the position of the cord as you turn.

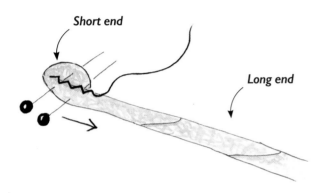

Fig. 5

5. Continue stitching and coiling the fabric around in a spiral. Hold the cord in your left hand and turn the coil clockwise with your right hand, lowering the needle and raising the presser foot to turn the work (Fig. 6).

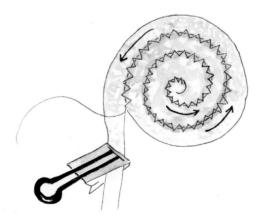

Fig. 6

6. To join a new fabric strip, trim the old and the new strips parallel to the selvedge. Tuck the new end between the cord and the old end, continue to wrap the fabric around the cord and secure again with the clip (Fig. 7).

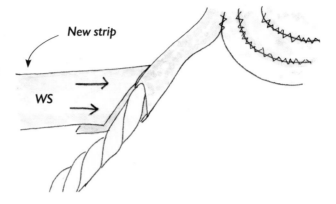

Fig. 7

7. Continue in Mosaic Bloom until the work measures 14cm (5½in). Change to strips of Provençal for another 2.5cm (1in). The work will measure 19cm (7½in) across.

8. Change back to Mosaic Bloom for a further 2.5cm (1in). The work will measure 24cm (9½in) across. Cut the thread and turn the work over.

TIP

If you are left-handed you may find it more comfortable to use the opposite hand. With a bit of practise you should find a method that suits you.

9. With Provençal, begin to build the sides of the bowl by keeping your left hand under the coiled base and lifting it to control the angle of the sides. The higher you hold the base as you coil, the steeper the sides of the bowl will become (Fig. 8).

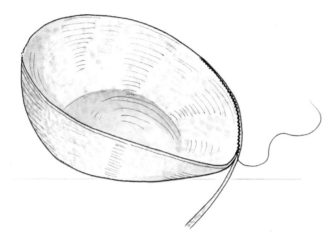

Fig. 8

9. After working with Provençal for 5cm (2in), change to Mosaic Bloom and work 2cm (¾in).

10. Change back to Provençal and work a further 5cm (2in). The bowl should stand at about 10cm (4in) high. Cut the covered cord and trim away 2cm (¾in) of cord. To finish, wrap the fabric over the cord end without creating too much bulk and stitch it to the bowl.

CHANGE YOUR STYLE!

Now you have learnt how to make three dimensional pieces with fabric coil work, start thinking creatively and you can not only change the fabric to suit your decor, but also change the shape of your bowl. Remember, if you hold the base higher when building your sides, the sides will be steeper. You could also change the shape of the base – why not try an oval or even a rectangle.

Change Your Style using Amy Butler Hapi, Heart Bloom in Rose and Tapestry Rose in Sapphire.

Cover-It-Up Food Cover

COVER-IT-UP FOOD COVER

Keep those pesky flies away from your delicious treats with a handy food cover, but make sure it's pretty. This project gives an old, drab food cover a new lease of life, or if you don't have an old one to hand you can pick one up very cheaply at a good home store.

If you follow the instructions given here carefully, you'll find these food covers are surprisingly easy to make and will look perfect on your picnic table or kitchen counter, keeping the cake and snacks safe.

YOU WILL NEED

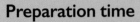

The finished cover will measure 35cm (14in) across and 20cm (8in) high.

- Food cover
- 60cm (23½in) of **Camelia** in *Butter*
- Coats cotton thread in white
- Masking tape
- Pattern paper
- Pinking shears

Preparation time

30 minutes

Sewing time

2 hours

Camelia in Butter

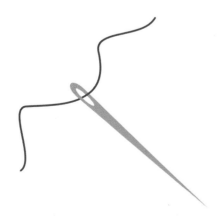

PREPARING YOUR FABRIC

Cutting the pattern

Draw a line on the bottom edge of the pattern paper and place the bottom edge of one side of the food cover (in the open position) on the line. Draw around the side (you may need to roll the side as you draw it if the side not sit flat on the surface). This creates the pattern for one side of the cover. Add a 1.5cm (⅝in) seam allowance all the way around (Fig. 1).

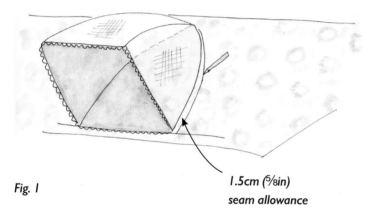

Fig. 1

1.5cm (⅝in)
seam allowance

Cutting the fabric

* Using the paper pattern, cut four pieces out of Camelia in Butter so that the print matches on all four sections.

* Cut four 6cm (2½in) square pieces from Camelia in Butter for the wire pockets.

* Cut four 4cm (1½in) wide strips using pinking shears, from the remaining fabric for the frills. These will each be approx 60cm (23½in) long.

MAKING THE COVER

1. Pin two of the main sections together with right sides (RS) facing. Try to match the pattern. Stitch to make a side seam, stopping 2cm (¾in) from the top point. Repeat with the other two sections, so you have two halves. Pin and match the two halves together and stitch to make both seams, stopping short of the top point.

Making the frill

2. Place the four frill strips in a row with the RS facing the same way and stitch the short ends together to create a circle. Fold the circle in half lengthways and finger crease to give a central guide. Set your machine to a long stitch length and, with the tension slightly loose, stitch two rows of gathering stitches either side of the central guide.

Wire pockets

3. With each 6cm (2½in) square piece, fold the sides into the centre (Fig. 2) then turn 90 degrees and fold in half again (Fig. 3.

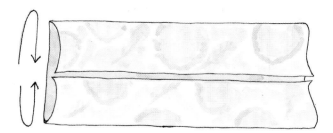

Fig. 2

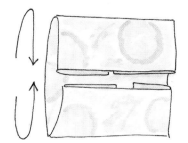

Fig. 3

4. Take a wire pocket and with the raw edges at the bottom, position it in one of the bottom corners of the cover at the seam. Stitch either side of the seam, wrapping the pocket around the seam.

Attaching the frill

5. Draw up the threads so that the frill is approximately the same length as the lower edge. Pin the frill to the RS lower edge of the cover, 1.5cm (⅝in) from edge. Stitch along the centre of the frill (Fig. 4).

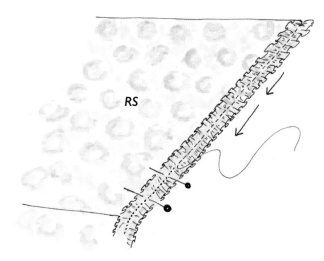

RS

Fig. 4

> ## TIP
> *If you have enough fabric, you could cut the frill strips on the bias.*

6. Turn under the seam allowance (this will cover the raw edge to form the hem) and stitch in place from the RS, holding back the frill as you go (Fig. 5).

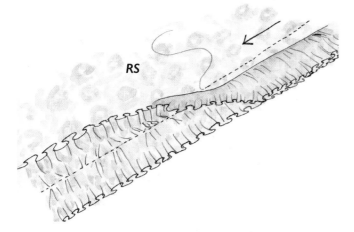

Fig. 5

7. Remove the old cover from its wire frame – you will have to unscrew the top part (connecter) and cover the sharp ends of the wires with a little masking tape to prevent them from working their way through the new fabric. Place the new cover over the frame – you may need to trim the top of the cover to get the connecter through. Place each wire in its pocket (Fig. 6) and replace the screw threaded cover.

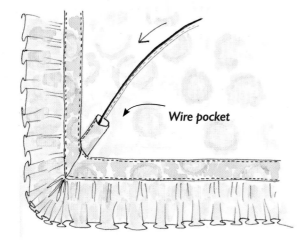

Wire pocket

Fig. 6

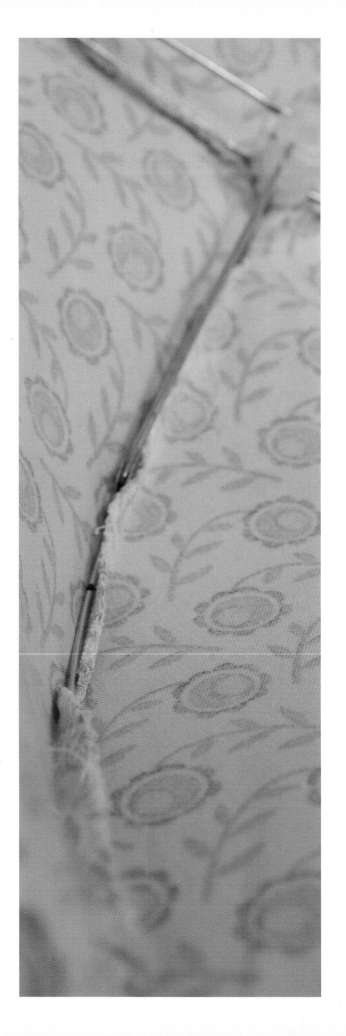

CHANGE YOUR STYLE!

As well as a change of fabric why not add a second set of frills. Create two layers of frills by stitching them on top of one another and then fluffing them up a bit so both can be seen. Make the lower layer a contrasting fabric so that it peeps out from beneath the main print.

Change Your Style using Amy Butler Hapi, Flowering Buds in Emerald.

LAZY LAP QUILT

LAZY LAP QUILT

Some days were created for lounging around, and having a selection of pretty quilts to snuggle up in are a must. The simple brickwork pattern in this design is fantastic for showing off a selection of bright and cheery fabrics. Follow the design shown here or get creative and try your own fabric combinations.

Once you've made one of these quilts you'll be making more as gifts or just so that you can have one in every room for extra cosiness!

YOU WILL NEED

The finished quilt will measure 96 x 132cm (37¾ x 52in).

Blocks

- 25cm (10in) of **Mosaic Bloom** in *Teal*
- 25cm (10in) of **Mosaic Bloom** in *Sunset*
- 25cm (10in) of **Houndstooth** in *Butter*
- 25cm (10in) of **Lily Pad** in *Butter*
- 25cm (10in) of **Provençal** in *Sunset*
- 25cm (10in) of **Camelia** in Butter

Backing and blocks

- 160cm (63in) of **Bold Bouquet** in *Teal*

Borders, blocks and binding

- 100cm (39⅓in) of **Aztec** in *Teal*
- 140cm (55in) of **Domino** in *Sunset*

Other

- 100 x 150cm (39⅓ x 59in) of quilt wadding (batting)
- Coats cotton thread in white x 3
- Small safety pins
- Masking tape

Preparation Time

1 hour

Sewing Time

6 hours

PREPARING YOUR FABRIC

Cutting the fabric

Blocks

- Cut two 9cm (3½in) wide strips from the width of the fabric in Mosaic Bloom in Teal (9 blocks).

- Cut two 9cm (3½in) wide strips from the width of the fabric in Mosaic Bloom in Sunset (6 blocks).

- Cut two 9cm (3½in) wide strips from the width of the fabric in Houndstooth in Butter (10 blocks).

- Cut two 9cm (3½in) wide strips from the width of the fabric in Lily Pad in Butter (10 blocks).

- Cut two 9cm (3½in) wide strips from the width of the fabric in Provençal in Sunset (10 blocks).

- Cut two 9cm (3½in) strips from the width of the fabric in Camelia in Butter (9 blocks).

- Cut each strip mentioned above into 16.5cm (6½in) blocks. The number of blocks you will need are shown in brackets.

Backing and blocks

- Cut a 100cm (39⅓in) piece from the length from Bold Bouquet in Teal. This is the backing.

- Cut the remaining smaller piece into thirteen 9 x 16.5cm (3½ x 6½in) blocks.

Borders and blocks

- Ensuring that the pattern sits straight across the width when folded, cut six 9cm (3½in) wide strips from Aztec in Teal, across the width, positioning so that the design sits in the middle of the strips, identical on each strip.

- Cut two of these strips into 16.5cm (6½in) blocks (creating ten blocks). This will leave two 30cm (00in) pieces which can be joined to two of the remaining strips to create the long border strips. The other two remaining strips will be the shorter border strips.

Binding, borders and blocks

- For the thin border, cut four 2cm (¾in) wide strips from across the width of Domino in Sunset. Cut two side borders to a length of 115.5cm (45½in) and cut two shorter borders to a length of 77.5cm (30½in) for the top and bottom.

- For the binding, cut four 5cm (2in) wide strips from across the width of Domino in Sunset.

- Cut two 9cm (3½in) wide strips from across the width of Domino in Sunset, then cut into six 16.5cm (6½in) blocks.

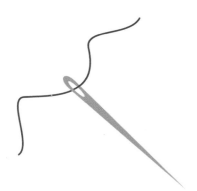

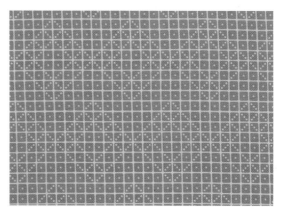

Domino in Sunset

Mosaic Bloom in Teal

Provençal in Sunset

Mosaic Bloom in Sunset

Aztec in Teal

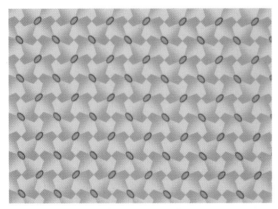

Houndstooth in Butter

Bold Bouquet in Teal

Lily Pad in Butter

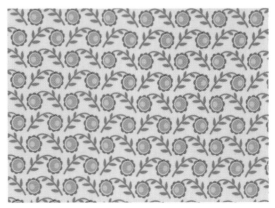

Camelia in Butter

PLANNING YOUR QUILT

Arrange the blocks in horizontal rows as shown in the plan (Fig. 1). The rows will alternate between having six blocks and five blocks.

Fig. 1

MAKING YOUR QUILT

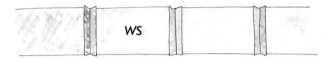

1. Attach each row of blocks together with a 6mm (¼in) seam allowance. When you have 15 complete rows, press the seams open (Fig. 2).

Fig. 2

2. With row 1 right side (RS) facing, place row 2 RS together, so that a vertical seam in row 2 sits between two of the seams in row 1, creating a brickwork pattern. The third row is in the same position as row 1. Keep joining the rows in this sequence until all the rows have been attached. Press all the seams to one side and trim off the excess from the sides (Fig. 3).

Fig. 3

Borders

3. Take the thin Domino borders and pin them to the quilt top, RS together. Do the sides first and then the top and bottom edges. Stitch in place (Fig. 4).

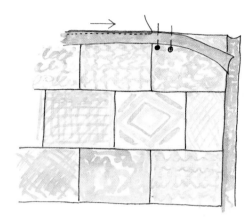

Fig. 4

4. Join the Aztec border strips, matching the pattern at the seams to create the long borders. Attach the borders to the quilt, long sides first (Fig. 5), then the two shorter pieces to the top and bottom. Press the seams towards the middle.

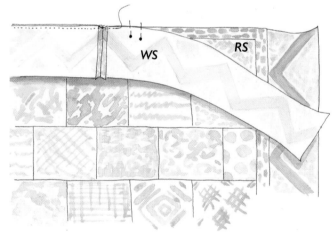

Fig. 5

5. Layer the quilt. Make sure that the grain of each layer is square when you place it down on the worktable. Start with the backing fabric RS down, place the wadding (batting) on top, then the quilt top, RS facing. Hold each layer in place with masking tape.

6. Using small safety pins, join the layers together at regular intervals close to the seams that you are going to quilt. Stitch in the ditch across all the horizontal seams and around the inner Domino border. Trim the wadding (batting) and the backing fabric to the edges of the quilt.

7. Join the Domino binding strips and pin to the quilt (Fig 6). Mitre the binding at each corner and stitch in place (Fig. 7). Press the binding and fold it over the edge of the quilt before pinning, and slip or ladder stitch in place on the RS (Fig. 8).

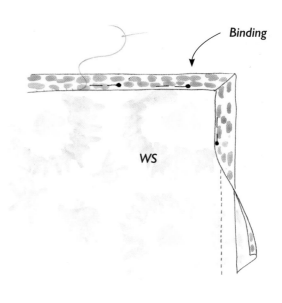

Fig. 8

8. Finish off by sewing any loose thread ends into the wadding (batting) in the quilt. Press the quilt, paying close attention to the binding to ensure you achieve a good, crisp finish.

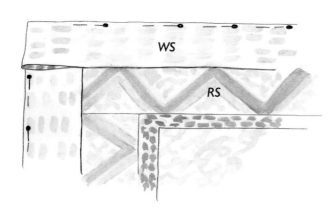

Fig. 6

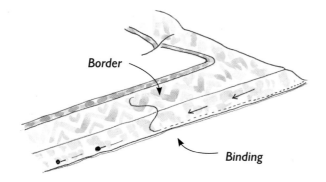

Fig. 7

TIP

If you don't want to use safety pins, you can either tack (baste) from the centre outwards, or use a basting gun which will secure the layers with plastic tags.

Change Your Style!

Who wouldn't be cosy under the warm colours of this stunning lap quilt? You can get very creative with your fabric choices here as the brickwork design is simple enough to tackle, even if it's your very first quilt. Just make sure you sew all your seams straight and quilt and bind it neatly, and you'll have a quality piece that will last for years to come. Play around with different fabrics and colours to achieve a look that will suit your own taste and decor.

Change Your Style using Amy Butler Hapi, Heart Bloom in Rose, Glow in Navy, Camel Blanket in Blush, Camel Blanket in Cloud, Oasis in Riverstone, Oasis in Azure, Oasis in Ocean and Oasis in Honeysuckle.

COMFY KITCHEN SEAT PADS

COMFY KITCHEN SEAT PADS

Encourage family time by making the kitchen chairs the most comfortable seats in the house! These seat pads will ensure that everyone stops to chat while dinner is being prepared and tea on your lap will be a thing of the past.

You can create your pattern to suit any size or shape kitchen chair and this design incorporates handy straps to hold them securely in place.

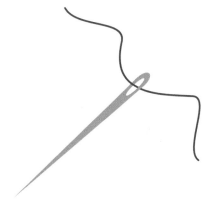

YOU WILL NEED

Makes two seat pads to fit any standard kitchen chair.

- 150cm (59in) of **Bold Bouquet** in *Deep Water*
- 50cm (20in) of **Bold Bouquet** in *Asparagus*
- 25cm (10in) of sew-in hook and loop fastening
- 65cm (25½in) zips x 2
- 7m (23ft) of 3mm (⅛in) piping cord
- Coats cotton thread no. 2336 x 2
- Pattern paper
- Fire retardant foam the size of the cushion x 2
- 100cm (39⅓in) of polyester upholstery wadding
- 100cm (39⅓in) of stockinette
- Adjustable zipper foot
- Sharp knife for cutting foam

Preparation Time
30 minutes

Sewing Time
2 hours

Bold Bouquet in Deep Water

Bold Bouquet in Asparagus

PREPARING YOUR FABRIC

Making the pattern

With the pattern paper placed at the back of the chair, crease the paper all the way around the edge of the seat to obtain the shape. Fold the paper in half to ensure the pattern is symmetrical and cut it out.

Draw around the pattern on the foam and cut with a sharp knife. Make long straight cuts. You can shape any rounded corners with some long sharp scissors (Fig. 1). Cover the foam with the polyester upholstery wadding as if you were wrapping a parcel. Then cover it with stockinette and pull tight so there are no wrinkles. Stitch so that it is flat and not bumpy (Fig. 2).

Fig. 1

Fig. 2

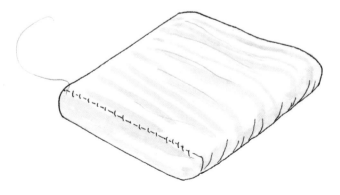

Cutting the fabric

Using your paper pattern, add a 1.5cm (⅝in) seam allowance and cut out four pieces from Bold Bouquet in Deep Water. If the fabric has an obvious directional design, make sure that you pin the pattern on the fabric correctly with the top of the pattern at the back edge of the cushion (Fig. 3).

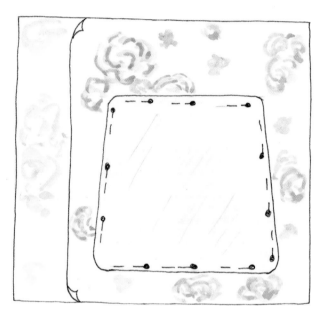

Fig. 3

- Cut two 8cm (3¼in) wide strips from across the width of Bold Bouquet in Deep Water for the front welts (cushion sides).

- Cut two 12 x 65cm (4½ x 25½in) wide strips from Bold Bouquet in Deep Water for the back welts.

- Cut four 8 x 22cm (3¼ x 8½in) strips from Bold Bouquet in Deep Water for the straps.

- Cut 7m (23ft) of 4cm (1½in) wide bias strips from Bold Bouquet in Asparagus.

SEWING THE CHAIR COVER

1. Begin by joining the bias strips. Trim the ends of each strip to a 45 degree angle, (when facing the same way up the ends must lie in the same direction).

2. Place the strips right sides (RS) together, so that the short ends overlap to form a 'V' at each side of the seam. Use a small stitch length to join the strips from one end to the other. Trim the seams to 5mm (¼in) and press open.

3. Lay the strips, wrong sides (WS) facing upwards and place the piping cord on top. Fold over the fabric and pin in the direction that you are sewing. Using an adjustable zipper foot, sew close but not tight to the piping cord. When you get to the end, cut the piping cord.

4. With your main fabric RS facing and starting at the back of the cushion, pin the piping in place. The edge of the piping should meet the edge of the cushion. Clip into the seam allowance if necessary.

5. When you get back to the beginning, cut the piping cord 3cm (1¼in) longer. Trim away enough cord so that it just meets the other end. Fold in the edge of the fabric and wrap around the other end of the piping. Repeat on the other three pieces.

Back welt and zip

6. Cut the back welts in half along the length of the fabric. On the lower half, place the zip tape to the RS of the fabric and pin and stitch in place. Stitch close to the zip teeth. Turn the fabric back and crease. Top stitch close to the fold (Fig. 4).

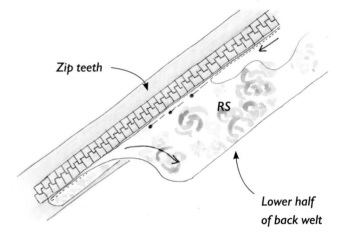

Zip teeth

RS

Lower half of back welt

Fig. 4

7. Place the other side of the zip tape to the top part of the welt and pin and stitch in place (Fig. 5).

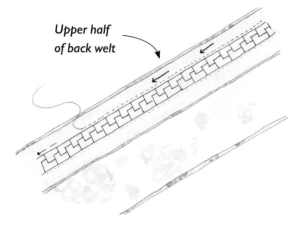

Upper half of back welt

Fig. 5

8. Using the front welt section as a guide for the finished width, place the lower edge of the back welt to the edge of the front welt and adjust the top edge of the back welt so that it is lined up with the top edge of the front welt. There will be a small amount of extra fabric. Fold this excess over the zip teeth (the fold should just cover the zip and top stitching of the lower half of the welt) and pin in place to the zip tape. Remove the front welt section and top stitch 1cm (½in) from the fold (Fig 6).

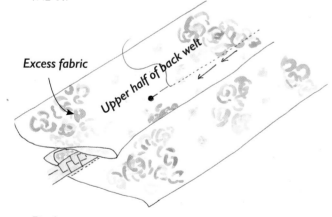

Excess fabric

Upper half of back welt

Fig. 6

9. Pin one short end of the front welt to the short end of the back welt that has the zip slider. Pin and stitch the two welts together. Press seam towards the front welt.

10. Find the centre of the back welt (keep the front welt to the right) and the centre of the back of the seat, and pin together. Pin on the seam line to the left, towards the beginning of the welt, up to 8cm (3in) from the end and then in the other direction, all the way round the cover.

11. Join the welt so that it fits snugly to the cover. Using an adjustable zipper foot, stitch all the way around. Attach the second side by first matching the corners and then pinning in place, then pin in between (Fig. 7). Stitch in place.

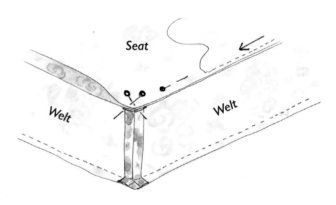

Seat

Welt

Welt

Fig. 7

TIP

When attaching piping, I often find that a normal piping foot is too small for anything over a few millimetres so I like to use an adjustable zipper foot instead.

Straps

12. Fold the strap in half along the length, RS facing, and stitch from either end, leaving an opening of 5cm (2in) halfway along the long side. Cut the corners (Fig. 8), finger press the seams open and turn through the opening. Hand stitch the opening closed and press.

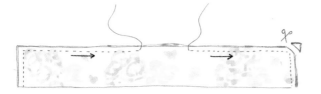

Fig. 8

13. Place one half of the hook and loop fastening on one end and stitch in place (Fig. 9). Place the other half at the other end on the opposite side and stitch in place.

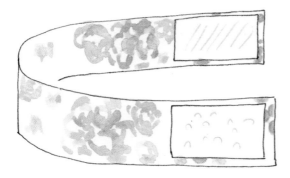

Fig. 9

14. Position the straps at the back corners of the cushion, so that the top part of the strap (the fastening that will overlap the other end) is pointing to the front of the cushion (Fig. 10). Being very careful not to stitch across the zip, stitch a small rectangle to firmly hold the strap in place. Repeat with the second strap, reversing the direction of the fastening overlap, again so that the top part points towards the middle of the zipped section.

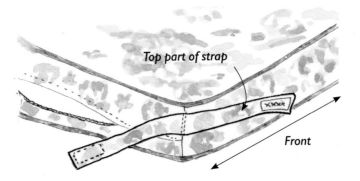

Top part of strap

Front

Fig. 10

15. Insert the foam to complete the cushion. Repeat the process to make the second seat pad.

61

Change Your Style!

Inside or out, loose chair seat covers are a quick, easy way to reinvent kitchen, garden or conservatory chairs. You can change the shape of the cushion and adjust the position of the straps to suit your own furniture, or if you just want to freshen up exisiting seat pads then use the old ones and just make new covers for them.

Change Your Style using Amy Butler Hapi, Camel Blanket in Blush and Camel Blanket in Cloud.

Country Kitchen Table Mats

COUNTRY KITCHEN TABLE MATS

Handmade and fabric tableware are sure to give your kitchen some country style. These mats are so simple to make, you'll be running sets up for every season and occasion. They would also make a lovely housewarming gift and don't require reams of fabric. The heat resistant wadding (batting) makes them a practical as well as a beautiful choice for your kitchen table.

The clever reversible design means you can mix and match to suit your mood and the occasion.

YOU WILL NEED

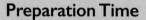

Makes a set of two table mats, each measuring 40 x 30cm (16 x 12in)

- 50cm (20in) of **Lily Pad** in *Deep Water*
- 50cm (20in) of **Mosaic Bloom** in *Deep Water*
- 50cm (20in) of **Houndstooth** in *Asparagus*
- 40cm (16in) of heat resistant wadding (batting)
- Coats cotton thread no. 9241

Preparation Time
30 minutes

Sewing Time
2 hours

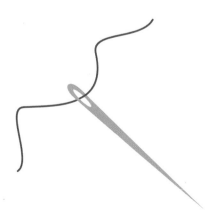

Lily Pad in Deep Water

Mosaic Bloom in Deep Water

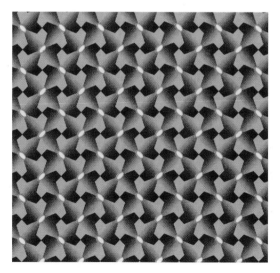

Houndstooth in Asparagus

PREPARING YOUR FABRIC

Cutting the pattern

Fold a 50 x 40cm (20 x 16in) piece of paper in half and draw a line 4.5cm (1¾in) from the fold. Fold in half again. At the intersection of the crease and the line, draw a semicircle from this point.

Cutting the fabric

- Using the paper pattern, cut two pieces in Mosaic Bloom.

- Cut two pieces in Lily Pad.

- Cut two pieces of wadding (batting).

- Cut 240 x 4cm (94½ x 1½in) bias strips of Houndstooth, positioning the print as shown in Fig. 1.

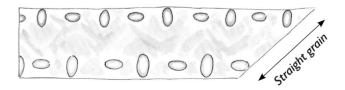

Fig. 1

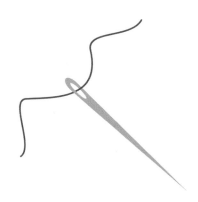

SEWING THE TABLE MATS

1. Join the bias strips together. Place right sides (RS) together and pin and stitch from one 'V' to the other 'V', using a small stitch length (Fig. 2).

4. Fold the binding over the edge and turn it under. Binding should be 1cm (0.4in) wide. Pin and slip or ladder stitch in place to finish (Fig. 4).

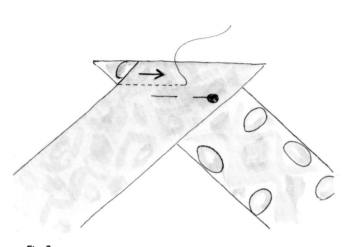

Fig. 2

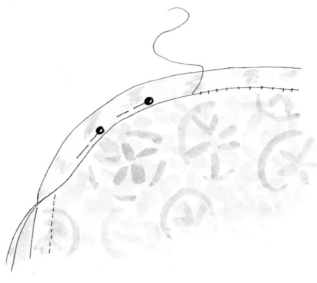

Fig. 4

2. Layer the table mats. Place the backing RS down, then the heat resistant wadding (batting) and then the top fabric, RS facing. Pin all the way around and tack (baste) in place.

3. Pin the bias binding around the edge, 1cm (½in) in and join the ends on the bias (Fig. 3). Stitch all the way around (Fig. 3).

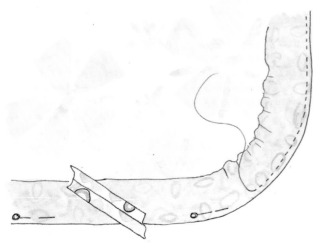

Fig. 3

> **TIP**
>
> *Very slightly stretch the binding as you pin it to the table mat then the outside edge will sit flat when you slip stitch it down on the reverse side.*

CHANGE YOUR STYLE!

I love these floral mats and why not create a complete set with coordinating table runner and napkins. Adjust the shape and dimensions to suit your table and use the same method as for the table mats. You could finish the look with a coordinating or contrasting coilwork bowl.

Change Your Style using Amy Butler Hapi, Sunflowers in Leaf and Oasis in Azure.

Keep-It-Cosy Draught Excluder

KEEP-IT-COSY DRAUGHT EXCLUDER

Nothing ruins a cosy night in more than a chilly draught running through the house. But stitch up a stylish draught excluder and that won't be a problem! All your rooms can now be extra cosy and snug.

This draught excluder not only looks good but is practical too, with a handy liner to keep the polystyrene beads where they should stay.

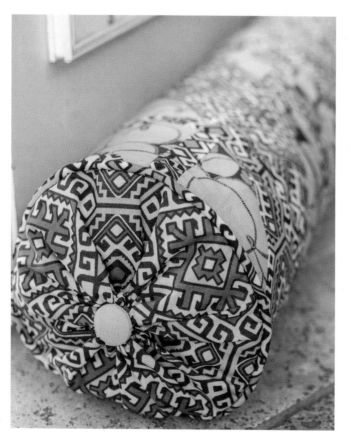

YOU WILL NEED

The finished draught excluder will measure 80cm (31½in) in length

- 70cm (27½in) of **Bold Bouquet** in *Deep Water*
- 70cm (27½in) of **Bold Bouquet** in *Asparagus*
- 70cm (27½in) of **Camelia** in *Apricot*
- 75cm (29½in) zips x 2
- 110cm (43⅓in) of 3mm (⅛in) piping cord
- 0.06 cu/m (2 cu/ft) of polystyrene beads
- Self cover buttons x 2
- Coats cotton thread no. 2336 x 2
- 100cm (39⅓in) calico for liner

Other

- Adjustable zipper foot
- Rotary cutter
- Cutting mat
- Ruler

Preparation Time

1 hour

Sewing Time

4 hours

Bold Bouquet in Deep Water

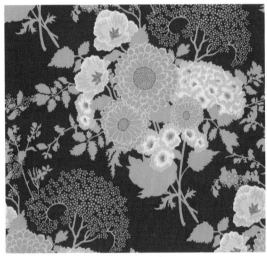

Bold Bouquet in Asparagus

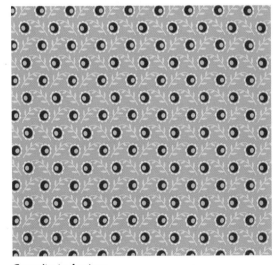

Camelia in Apricot

PREPARING YOUR FABRIC

Cutting your fabric

Squares and triangles

- Cut fourteen 12.5cm (4¾in) squares from each of Bold Bouquet in Deep Water and Asparagus. Cut each square diagonally to form two triangles.

Sashing strips

- From Camelia in Apricot, cut six strips 3 x 47cm (1¼ x 18½in) for the long sashing strips.

- Cut 21 strips, 3 x 12.5cm (1¼ x 4¾in) for the short sashing strips.

- Cut two strips, 4 x 47cm (1½ x 18½in) for the piping (these could be bias strips if you have enough fabric).

- Cut two strips 9 x 47cm (3½ x 18½in) for the wider sashing strips.

End Pieces

- From Bold Bouquet in Deep Water, cut two rectangles, 50 x 12cm (19⅝ x 4¾in).

Liner

- From the 100cm (40in) of calico, cut two rectangles, 50 x 16cm (20 x 6¼in).

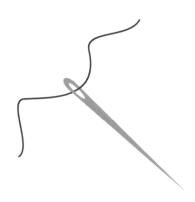

SEWING THE DRAUGHT EXCLUDER

Blocks

1. Sew two contrasting triangles of fabric together to form a square and press the seams open. Repeat until all the triangles have been stitched together.

2. Position the square blocks as shown in the piecing plan (Fig. 1).

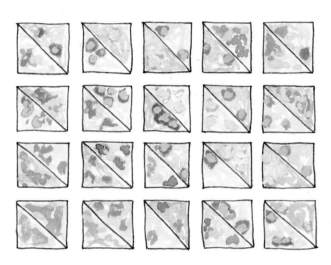

Fig. 1

3. Attach a short sashing strip between each square to form a row of seven blocks and six sashing strips. Press the seams open. Join each row to a long sashing strip, pressing the seams towards the centre of the sashing strip.

4. Attach the two wider sashing strips along the long edges (Fig. 2). Take one long edge and bring it up to the other long edge, right sides (RS) facing. Stitch a short seam, 1.5cm (⅝in) in for 5cm (2in) at both ends (Fig. 3).

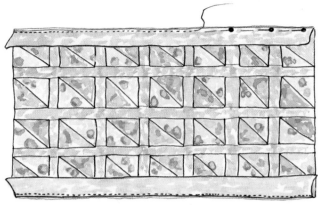

Fig. 2

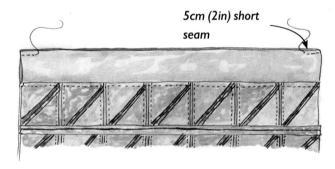

5cm (2in) short seam

Fig. 3

TIP

Be very accurate with your cutting. Use a rotary cutter, cutting mat and ruler and all your pieces will fit together beautifully.

5. Fold the seam allowance back and crease (Fig. 4). Place the zip over the back of the opening and pin to the seam allowance only (Fig. 5).

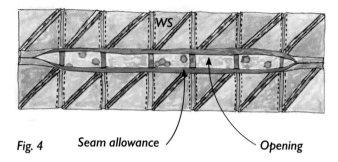

Fig. 4   Seam allowance   Opening

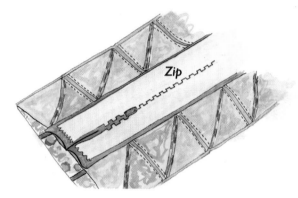

Fig. 5

6. Stitch the zip in place. Stitch close to the zip teeth on both sides. From the RS, crease the fabric so that the edges meet. Pin and stitch in the ditch alongside the zip sashing (Fig. 6).

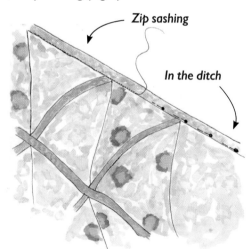

Fig. 6

7. Cover the piping cord with the two 4cm (1½in) strips of fabric (these could be bias strips if you have enough fabric). Pin and stitch to either end of the cover using an adjustable zipper foot.

8. Using the small rectangles of Bold Bouquet, fold one in half and stitch the short sides to form a circle. Attach one end to one end of the cover, RS facing. Run a gathering thread all the way around the other edge. Draw up and stitch firmly in place. Repeat at the other end of the cover.

9. Cover two buttons with Camelia in Apricot. Stitch a button in place at the centre of each gathered end.

Making the liner

10. Take the piece of calico and fold in half lengthways. Leaving a 70cm (27½in) opening for the zip, sew a seam either end of the zip position. To insert the zip, place the zip tape RS facing to the raw edge of the liner and pin and stitch in place. Repeat on the other side of the zip. Gather both ends of the cylinder. Pull up the thread and securely stitch in place.

11. Open the zip and fill with polyester beads and close the zip as the liner fills up. Do not overfill as the draught excluder needs a little movement to sit against the door snugly. Insert the filled liner into your draught excluder and plump up to finish.

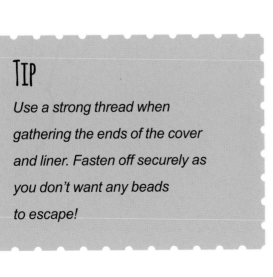

TIP

Use a strong thread when gathering the ends of the cover and liner. Fasten off securely as you don't want any beads to escape!

Change Your Style!

A bright draught excluder is just what you need on a chilly day to brighten things up a little! Amy Butler's fabric is sure to warm any room and this version will add a little homespun style to the atmosphere. You'll be snuggling up for an early night in no time!

Change Your Style using Amy Butler Hapi, Camel Blanket in Blush, Camel Blanket in Cloud and Heart Bloom in Rose.

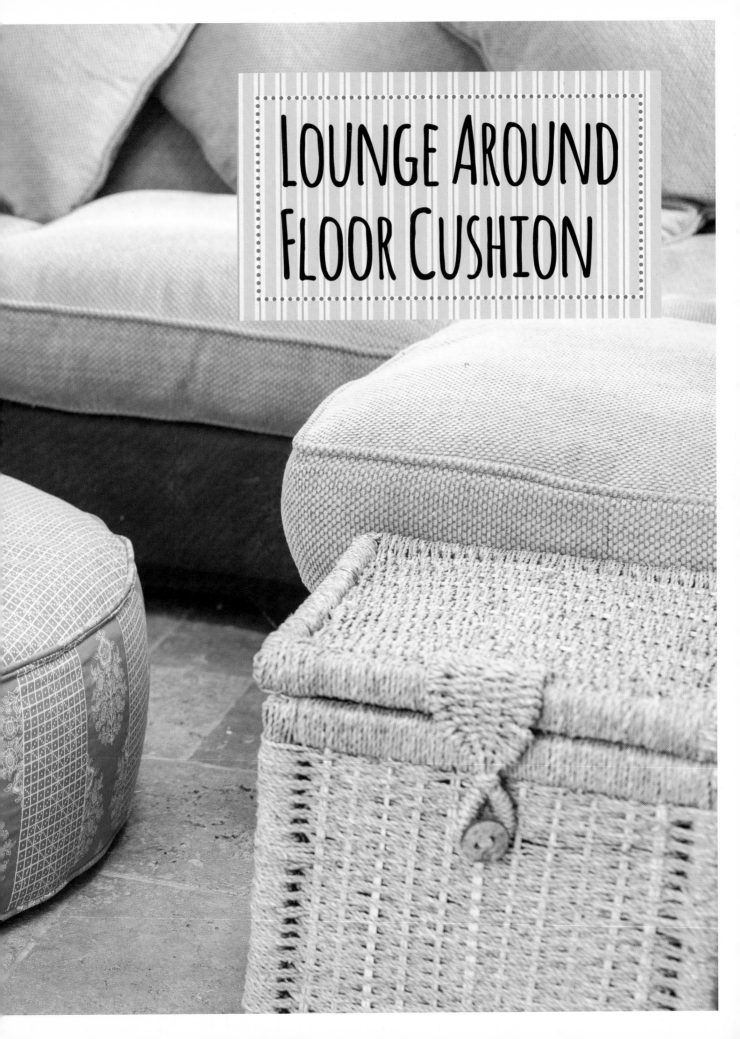

Lounge Around Floor Cushion

LOUNGE AROUND FLOOR CUSHION

A happy house is one full of people and unexpected guests which means that additional seating is a must. Floor cushions are the ideal solution for parties, movie nights and extra visitors.

You can whip this cushion up in an afternoon so no-one need sit on the floor again.

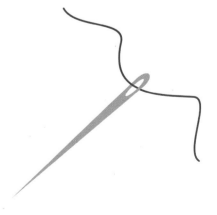

YOU WILL NEED

The finished floor cushion will measure 90cm (35½in) across and 23cm (9in) high.

- 100cm (39⅓in) of **Mosaic Bloom** in *Sunset*
- 180cm (71in) of **Domino** in *Sunset*
- 180cm (71in) of **Provençal** in *Sunset*
- 200cm (78¾in) of calico for the liner
- 100cm (39⅓in) zip
- 70cm (27½in) zip
- 0.18 cu/m (6.35 cu/ft) bag of polystyrene beads
- Coats cotton thread in white
- Adjustable zipper foot

Preparation Time

1 hour

Sewing Time

3 hours

Mosaic Bloom in Sunset

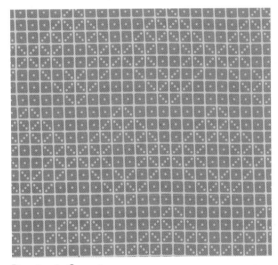

Domino in Sunset

Provençal in Sunset

PREPARING YOUR FABRIC

Cutting the pattern

A 1.5cm (⅝in) seam allowance has been included throughout.

- For the top and bottom, draw a circle with a 92cm (36¼in) diameter.

- For the side sections, draw a rectangle that is 26cm (10½in) high and 13cm (5in) wide.

Cutting the fabric

- For the top and bottom panels, cut one circle each from Mosaic Bloom and Domino.

- Cut 14 side panels from Domino.

- Cut 14 side panels from Provençal.

- Cut 300 x 4cm (118 x 1½in) bias strips from Provençal.

- From the lining fabric, cut two circle pieces.

- From the lining fabric, cut two 26 x 146cm (10½ x 57½in) pieces.

TIP

If the fabric has an obvious directional design, alternate the side panels so that they face up or down, making the cushion truly reversible!

SEWING THE CUSHION

1. Begin by joining the bias strips. Trim the ends of each strip to a 45 degree angle, (when facing the same way up the ends must lie in the same direction).

2. Place the strips right sides (RS) together, so that the short ends overlap to form a 'V' at each side of the seam. Use a small stitch length to join the strips from one end to the other (Fig. 1). Trim the seams to 5mm (¼in) and press open.

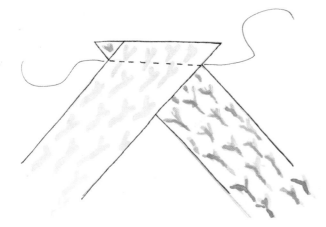

Fig. 1

3. Lay the strips, wrong sides (WS) facing and place the piping cord on top. Fold the fabric over the cord and pin it to the cord in the direction that you are sewing. Using an adjustable zipper foot, sew close but not tight to the cord (Fig. 2).

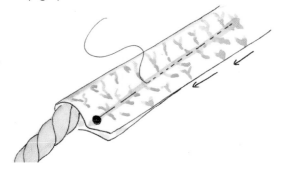

Fig. 2

4. Pin and machine stitch the piping to the RS of the top circular panel, around the edge. When you get back to the beginning, cut the piping so that it overlaps by 3cm (1.1in). Trim the cord to meet the other end of the cord and fold the fabric under (Fig. 3). Wrap the fabric around the other end of the piping and finish stitching to the top panel (Fig. 4). Repeat this to add piping to the bottom panel.

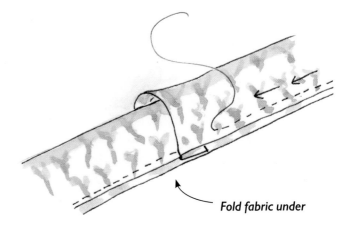

Fold fabric under

Fig. 3

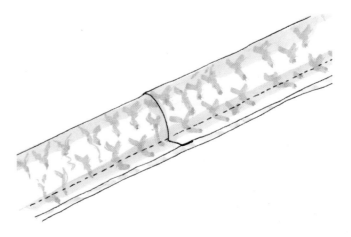

Fig. 4

5. Pin and stitch the side panels together, alternating the fabric (Fig. 5). If the design is directional, alternate between the pattern pointing up and down so the cushion can face either way. Press the seams open.

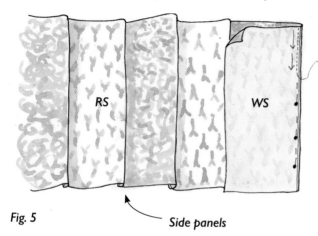

Fig. 5

Side panels

6. Attach the completed side panel to the top panel. Pin all the way around on the seam allowance or the side may not appear to fit exactly to the top panel. Stitch in place.

7. Pin the opposite edge of the side panel to the bottom panel. For a 100cm (39⅓in) length, cut little notches at regular intervals into the seam allowance so that you can match them up while inserting the zip.

8. Remove the pins in the notched section and stitch the bottom panel to the side panel around the remaining circumference, leaving the notched section open. Pin the zip so the edge of the tape and the edge of the seam allowance are together and sew in place. (Fig. 6). Fold the seam back to form a fold over the zip teeth by 0.5cm (¼in) and top stitch in place.

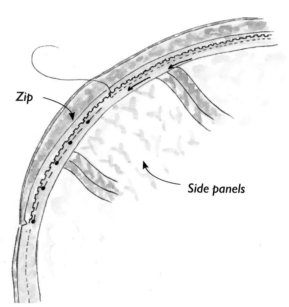

Zip

Side panels

Fig. 6

9. Fold the zip tape and seam allowance under, so that the edge of the fabric is just visible from the WS. Stitch in place.

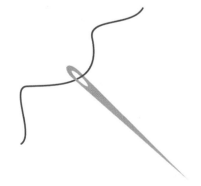

TIP

Polystyrene beads have a will of their own so enlist another pair of hands to help you fill the liner.

10. With the cover turned inside out, close the zip as much as you can and pin it to the remaining seam allowance on the bottom panel. Open the zip fully and pin and stitch the zip as close as you can to the piping cord (Fig. 7).

RS of the panel and sew in place. Repeat with the other side of the zip, matching the notches as you go to line up the top with the sides. Turn through to the RS and fill with the polystyrene beads. Place the liner inside the cover and plump up to finish.

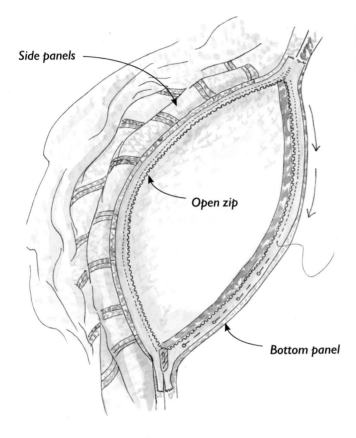

Side panels

Open zip

Bottom panel

Fig. 7

Making the liner

11. Join the two rectangles of calico together along the short edge to create a ring. Pin one edge of the side panel to one of the circles with RS facing. Stitch in place.

12. Pin the opposite edge of the side panel to the other circle, leaving a 70cm (27½in) opening for the zip. Cut little notches into the seam allowance so they can be matched up when inserting the zip. Remove the pins in the notched section and stitch the seam around the remaining circumference. Pin one half of the zip to the

89

CHANGE YOUR STYLE!

Everyone loves relaxing on a floor cushion. They are great when extra seating is required, or just for propping up your feet! This crazy Oasis design is perfect for a sun room or conservatory and with its easily removable cover is not difficult to launder.

Change Your Style using Amy Butler Hapi, Oasis in Ocean, Oasis in Honeysuckle and Oasis in Riverstone.

ABOUT THE AUTHOR

Margaret Rowan has been designing and sewing all kinds of projects since childhood, creating many unusual and creative outfits as a teenager for herself and her younger sisters!

This led her to a City and Guilds in Fashion and Textiles, and a degree from Camberwell School of Art and Craft in Textile Design and Printmaking.

Her love of making beautiful, functional projects has naturally taken her through a very interesting career, making and designing everything from wedding and ball gowns to soft furnishings for every kind of building - tiny cottages, stately homes and fabulous hotels.

As a passionate knitter she began working for Rowan Yarns in the mid 90s and this rekindled the workshop tutor inside her. After a year or two, she set up her own teaching studio and this led to writing her first book Stitch - The Complete Guide to Hand Sewing and Embellishing.

Teaching and encouraging other people to learn new skills is very important to her: "There is so much satisfaction in creating things for yourself, whatever form it takes. I hope this book will encourage and delight those who look inside and maybe take that first step in to the wonderful world of sewing!"

ACKNOWLEDGMENTS

A huge thank you goes to four very talented and lovely ladies: Emily Davies, my lovely, patient Editor; Susan Campbell for your amazing illustrations; and Vicki Walker who made such a beautiful job of the projects in the alternative colourways.

Last, but not least, my Mum, who passed away in 2013, who encouraged me to sew and never once said: 'Are you really going out in that?!'

Thank you to Janome for their support and for their wonderful sewing machine, the Memory Craft 9800 QCP. Fantastic!!

Thank you also to Coats Crafts for supplying all the delicious fabric, Sharon Brant for asking me to work on the book, and to Honor Head for all her help, support and fabulous organization!

SUPPLIERS

Coats Crafts UK
Green Lane Mill
Holmfirth
West Yorkshire HD9 2DX, UK
Tel: 01484 681881
www.makeitcoats.co.uk

Stitch Craft Create
Brunel House,
Forde Close,
Newton Abbot,
Devon TQ12 4PU, UK
Tel: 0844 880 5852
www.stitchcraftcreate.co.uk

INDEX

A DAVID & CHARLES BOOK
© F&W Media International, Ltd 2014

David & Charles is an imprint of F&W Media International, Ltd
Brunel House, Forde Close, Newton Abbot, TQ12 4PU, UK

F&W Media International, Ltd is a subsidiary of F+W Media, Inc
10151 Carver Road, Suite #200, Blue Ash, OH 45242, USA

Text and Designs © F&W Media International, Ltd 2014
Layout and Photography © F&W Media International, Ltd 2014

First published in the UK and USA in 2014

Margaret Rowan has asserted her right to be identified as author of this
work in accordance with the Copyright, Designs and Patents Act, 1988.

A catalogue record for this book is available from the British Library.

ISBN-13: 978-1-4463-0516-4 paperback
ISBN-10: 1-4463-0516-3 paperback

Printed in Italy by G. Canale & C S.p.A for:
F&W Media International, Ltd
Brunel House, Forde Close, Newton Abbot, TQ12 4PU, UK

10 9 8 7 6 5 4 3 2 1

Acquisitions Editor: Sarah Callard
Desk Editor: Honor Head
Project Editor: Emily Davies
Designer: Quail
Photographer: Jesse Wild
Styling: Quail Studio
Illustrator: Susan Campbell
Senior Production Controller: Kelly Smith

F+W Media publishes high quality books on a wide range of subjects.
For more great book ideas visit: www.stitchcraftcreate.co.uk